Just Hangin' Out!

A.L. Smith

DISCLAIMER:

All names used in this book other than that of
Author, Publisher and those mentioned in the
Dedication section are ficticious. Any resemblence
to anyone or anything is totally unintentional.
So, if anyone is insulted or otherwise upset in any
way by the writings here in this book, oh well, you
were told! It's Fiction!!

DEDICATION:

This book is dedicated to all Rednecks far and near. In the USA and abroad, wherever you may be! Hope you enjoy reading it!

I would also like to thank those who's sense of humor have inspired me for years and shown me what comedy can do for the sole. People such as my Grandfather, Richard Smith and those I don't even know like Jay Leno, Conan O'Brien, Howie Mandel, Jeff Foxworthy and many more of those comedians that I have enjoyed so much through the years.

The Westwood Redneck

Chains:

I've always like chains, especially those bright
silver and gold ones. I was even going to weld my
name on the back of my truck with silver ones until I
got this notice from the United States Postal Service
that said, "Chain letters are illegal!"

Letter to absentee landlord:

I'm writin you to give response
to last months mean ole letter
musta had somethin in yer craw
hope yer feelin better!

I cleaned up all the nasty stuff
the naybors said I had
to tell the truth and state the facts
it really weren't that bad!

As far as all the cars I got
a quarter acres plenty
they don't take up all that much space

6.

Hell I ain't got but twenty!

I moved them cars all around
and now they're neatly parked
Hell ya can't even see em
when ya drive by in the dark!

Ain't got but two trailers of beer cans
and they're both parked out back
an as far as the twoholer with the fridge
why that's my smokin shack!

If they think the grass is all too long
I got a damn good reason
by the time that I'm done fishin
it's always huntin season!

Now as for the trailer
the insides really nice
Oh yeah, summa the ceilin fell
but that only happened twice!

The trailers pretty level
and about as stable as can be
cause when I moved er in here
I leaned er right up aginst a tree!

Them three broke front windas
I covered up with plastic
so when yer lookin from the road
they really look fantastic!

The siding on the trailer
seems to be alright
summa the ends er flappin
but the rest is goodin tight!

The skirting that they mentioned
doesn't need no repair!
cause it's just like it always was
only half was ever there!

8.

Well that's about it
can't do no more this year
the family will be out workin
an I'll be a huntin deer!

Takin a dip:

There ain't nothing like opening a can
an takin out a big ole dip
an puttin that sucker in yer mouth
t'ween yer gums and bottom lip!

Ya git ya four or five napkins
an put em in a Dixie cup
then ya use the cup to spit in
til the tobacky's all used up!

Now there comes a time ya ain't got no cup
so ya spit in an ole beer can
so if yer gonna drink and ya don't stop and think
Ya better take it like a man!

After school meetin':

Otis finally got up the nerve to ask Sara Jean out

after school.

Sara Jean said, "I'm sorry, I'd like to but I can't. I

gotta go meet my Mama after school."

Otis then said, "Oh, well that's nice and don't you

be nervous now. I got ta meet my paw last year an

everything turned out great!"

Duck:

Just my luck. They told me to duck my head and

guess what that sucker did ta me as soon as I put er

up there!

Lights:

I went ta the hardware store ta git me some new

light switches.

The man showed me some switches and said, "These

are nice switches. See you can move em up and

down an they don't make no noise!"

I said. "That's stupid, how the hell am I supposed ta

Know if the light came on if I don't hear the click?!"

Name on belt:

Me and Darrell was sittin at our local bar drinkin' a cold beer, when these two city boys walked in n sat down.

Emmy Lou was waitin' on the tables and she was wearin' boots, tight blue jean (with her name on the back of her belt) an a halter top. Looked pretty sharp!

Anyway, she was real busy an had ta walk by em several times with drinks til she could git to em. They'd snicker and wisecrack every time she walked by.

Finally when she went to take their order, one of em said sarcastically, "Why do you have your name on the back of your belt, ya thinks it's cool?"

Emmy Lou came right back with, "The names there so that when I walk away from this table ya'll can see who's ass ya gotta kiss if yer gonna get a drink!

Out ridin':

Darrell and his wife had just come back from a two
week vacation and came over ta visit.

I was sittin' watchin' tv when they got there.

When they came in, Darrell's wife looked around
and then asked where my wife was.

I said, "I guess she's out back on one a them trails."

Then Darrell said, "I thought you said her horse died
a few days before we left fer vacation!"

I said, "Yep, and she's been a ridin' my ass every
day since!"

Bears:

I was told there has been a lot of bear sightings in
Michigan this winter! Brrrrrrrrr, seems those folks
would wanna keep ther clothes on this time a year!

Newmonia:

I went ta see Darrell at the hospital cause he had
newmonia. They told me Darrell was in "stable
condition".

12.

They were right! Every time Darrell sneezed while I was there, he'd go "uhuh-horshit!"

Them aint fish!:

Me and Darrell went on a fishin trip.

Darrell brought his boat and we went way out ta the middle of the lake early in the mornin'

I was sittin in the back of the boat and Darrell, sittin up front, decided ta cast his line way out there..

Well, he swung the pole back an caught his treble hook right in the crotch of my pants! As if that weren't bad enough he jerked it and it hit it's mark!

I yelled out and Darrell turned around with a shocked look on his face and said "Aw nuts!"

Just learnin!:

When I was just a little whipper-snapper, my Mama told my Daddy that he aughta take me out fishin with im.

So Daddy got me up at 4:30 in the mornin and we went ta this lake not far from home and Daddy and me got inta this little row boat and rowed out inta the lake.

This was fun, I'd never been fishin before! We rowed around on the lake til Daddy said "This looks like a good spot" and he threw the anchor out into the water.

Then, Daddy fixed up his pole and a little pole fer me. Then he put a worm on his hook and cast it out and said "First ya gotta throw yer bait waaaaaaaaaay out there."

I said, "Okay, Daddy and I grabbed the bait can and threw it waaaaaaaaaaaay out there!"

Daddy took me home!

Learnin ta drive:

Hank's daughter Mary Ann was just learnin ta drive and Hank didn't want er out on the roads yet, so he brought her over ta my place.

He asked if it would be alright fer her ta drive around the back pasture fer awhile til she got the hang of it.

14.

Well, we was out in the pasture an Mary Ann was
drivin all over the place. Zig zaggin around, hittin
the brakes, spinnin an all. Hank n me just watchin.
Then all of a sudden she started comin in our
direction, movin pretty fast! We started runnin n
dodgin back n forth but the next thing ya know, she
run right over my ass!

Hurt? Hell yeah it hurt! I paid three hunderd dollars
fer that donkey!

Snapper:

Me and Lester was drivin down the road all dressed
in our Sunday go ta meetin clothes, headed fer Ole
Amos' funeral.

All of a sudden we seen this big ole snappin turtle in
the middle of the road.

Well Lester loved turtle meat, so he told me ta stop
so's he could git it an throw it in the back a the
truck.

I stopped n Lester got out n picked up the turtle by
the tail. Well, the turtle retched out n snapped hold

the crotch of Lesters pants!

Lestered yelled and he pulled an he tugged an he tuggred an pulled but couldn't git the turtle off.

He got back in the truck an asked me, "How the hell do ya git these thangs off of ya?"

I said, "well they tell me ya gotta wait fer em ta go ta sleep an they'll let go."

Lester said, "Oh Hell!!"

Well, I started drivin an Lester kept a watchin that turtle.

We got ta the funeral home an the turtle still had a real good hold on Lesters crotch!

So we cut the head off the turtle, but the sucker still didn't let go!

Lester said, "What the hell am I gonna do now? I'm supposed ta do that youligy thing in about ten minutes! I caint go up there like this!"

I said, "Sure ya can Les, it might lighten things up a bit an if they ask, just tell em Lesters' little man there is wearin a turtle neck!"

16.

The boy loves his Uncle Jesse:

When my boy was six years old, I was sittin in the livin room watchin football one Sunday.

All of a sudden my boy come runnin thru the livin room headed fer the front door with his toy gun twixt his legs.

I said, "whoa boy, where ya goin so fast?"

The boy looked down at his gun and said, "Mama's takin us ta town an I'm ridin shotgun just like Uncle Jesse!"

Cookin problems:

Darrell's wife had been askin Darrell fer one a them ole wood cook stoves fer a long time.

Well, Darrell finally got tired a hearin it, so he built her one.

The first time she tried ta bake some bread the stove burnt ta the ground!

Busy bodies:

There was a big dance at the Grange Hall and just about everybody around was there, including the two old maid, Garland sisters, Clara and Esther.

Well, with this big dance goin on, my daughter decided this was a good time ta introduce her fiance ta everybody.

When she introduced him to the Garland sisters, Clara asked her what he did fer a livin.

"I'm a Taxidermist." he said.

Esther put her hanky up to her mouth and said, "Oh my!"

For the rest a the night, I heard the Garland sisters goin around whisperin ta all the ladies, "It's just like Wes and his wife to let their daughter get involved with a man like that, we hear those Taxidermists will mount anything!"

18.

Uhumm, great answer!:

The fifth grade teacher at our local school was askin questions of individual students on Friday.

When she came to little Jesse, she asked, "Jesse, if my husband was driving 40 miles an hour, how far could he go in a twelve hour period?"

Jesse said, "I don't know teacher, as far as you'll let im I spose!"

Lunch?:

Saturdy was a hot and breezy day.

I came inta the house and it was already past noon and I asked my wife, "Honey, when ya gonna start lunch? I'm starved!"

She said, "I don't know hon, it's hot in here and there is a nice breeze outside, can't we do it out on the pit?"

I said, "Okay, but then will ya start lunch?"

Bad Start?:

My nephew Jimmy and his girlfriend wanted ta elope ta Las Vegas and they wanted ta do it in a hurry!

Well, they couldn't afford a flight out ta Vegas, so crazy Jimmy went and hi-jacked a small plane and made the pilot take em ta Vegas!

They got married alright, but now the judge has sentenced em to 20 years each fer Jackelopin!

Good Excuse:

I've heard this excuse from people late fer weddins, work, dates, parties and who knows what all.

"I would have been here sooner, but I was runnin late!"

Explains everything don't it?

Never Learned!:

My daughter got married and moved out of state a couple years ago.

I got a call from my Son-in-Law the other day.

20.

He wanted ta let me know he had just come back from the hospital. My daughter was pregnant and he had taken her in early that mornin cause they thought she was gonna have the baby. He said it was just false labor.

I said, "Well, that don't surprise me none, we had trouble all through her school years with her usin improper contractions!"

Cheap Livin?:

My friend Hap is single and always tries ta live just as cheap as he can.

Well, Hap went n rented one of them 8X10 storage buildins fer fourty dollars a month.

Now he has a law suite agin the company cause they won't let im live there.

I think he has a good chance a winnin the suite tho, cause it says "Self Storage" right on the front of the buildin!

Sorry Doc!:

I had ta go the other day

ta see my famly fizishon.

And when the Doc came in the room

he caught me in a bad position!

He asked what I was doin and told

me ta explain toim

Why I was sittin there like that

an exactly what I was doin

I told im my insurance man called

an he was such a jerk

said he wouldn't cover my reck

cause I wasn't goin ta work!

He said since I was off road muddin

an ran into those fences

they wouldn't cover my ole truck

Or medical expenses!

22.

So I'm just sittin on this thing

waitin fer a line

So's I kin fax the man my ass

so he kin kiss it just one time!

Weddin':

Ya know, it would be nice if my daughter

an her mother would keep me up ta speed on things

around here! I knew my daughter was gittin married

an all, but I didn't know she was gittin married on

horseback til taday when they told me they was

headed out ta some fancy bridle shop!

No Account?:

The teacher was instructin the fifth grade class on

the test she was giving.

This test she said is multiple choice, so all you have

to do is put a check in the box next to the answer

you think is right.

Little Billy raised his hand and said, "Teacher can I

put exxes in the boxes instead? My paw says if he

ever catches me writin checks he'll whup my ass!"

Teeth?:
As far as dental hijean goes
my grandpaw didn't care
He was always more interested
in keepin up his hair.

So when he had the last one pulled
he didn't shed no tears.
He said, "it ain't nothin ta cry about.
They lasted fifty years!"

Now grandpaw's got some new teeth
but he doesn't use em much.
He says ther artificial and
ther nothin but a crutch!

When we come home from church on Sunday
he leaves em in the car.
Or if he decides ta bring em in

24.

He throws em in an ole fruit jar!

When grandmaw starts complainin
grandpaw says, Oh hush,
Them dang things ain't necessary
an ther just another thing ta brush!

He said, "I can eat corn on the cob,
apples, carrots n stuff.
Cause oncet you've eat as much as me
yer gums git pretty tough!"

Now I kinda agree with grandpaw
and the truth of the matter is
if I keep goin like I'm goin
I'll have new teeth just like his!

Oh Really!:
I went through my wifes closet the other night!
To be honest with ya, I didn't think she could throw
me that hard!!

This is my position on the Gun Issue:
There's been a real push from some
ta take away our guns.
But if we let em do that,
who will protect our sons?

It's never been the government
that did any of the fightin.
In fact when government gits involved
everything seems ta heighten!

It's always been the biggest part
of every country's dreams
to keep their people vulnerable
so they can carry out their schemes!

Now ya couldn't have a dictator
runnin the country by hisself
If every honest man
hand guns on his closet shelf!

26.

Can you imagine a country
overrun with beasts and even quail,
if every man caught with a gun
was locked up in a jail?

Now they want to put a shelf life
on every single bullet!
And be careful if ya have a license,
the government might just pull it!

When they tell us we're protected
and our troops are spread world wide,
We'll be here without our guns
and have no place ta hide!

But if ya need a place to go
somethin ta eat or a job,
Just don't worry yer little head
ask the government or the Mob!!

Shoppin':

We got our income tax check the other day, so I
asked my wife what she'd like ta do.

She said she'd like ta look over some new cars, so I
drove ta the top of the hill behind the car lot!

Waistin time (sing it Earle!)

I'm sittin on this bale a hay
watchin the tractor roll away
I see it go thru the hog pen
cause I forgot ta set the brake again
Yeah, I'm sittin here drinkin my beer
Wastin time

Left the house this mornin
headed out ta cut some hay
I had no one ta help me
seems like nothing seems ta go my way

I'm just sittin on this bale a hay
watchin the tractor roll away

28.

Just sittin here drinkin my beer
Wastin time

Looks like I gotta git the truck and some chains
all because I didn't use my brains
Didn't do what I should do
so ther's no one else ta blame

I'm just sittin here restin my bones
the damn flies won't leave me alone
All around the farm I roam
just ta work them fields alone

Yeah, I'm gonna sit on this bale a hay
watchin the tractor roll away
Just sit here drinkin my beer
Wastin time!

And why are ya mad:

Darrell's wife is mad as hell.

Their house was burglarized, so Darrell took his wife and went down to the Police station.

The Officer asked, "Can I help you?"

Before Darrell could say anything, his wife piped up and said, "I hope so, I've just been broken in!"

Darrell and the Police Officer rolled on the floor laughin'!

Owls?:

When I got home from work last night, my wife was in a really bad mood! When I asked her why she said, "Well, I had a lot a stuff I wanted ta do tommora, but thanks ta you and Darrell n yer big mouths, I gotta take yer grandson ta the Zoo cause he wants ta see some hooters!

30.

What can Uncle Sam do?

Ain't got no truck

and I ain't got no car

so I caint git ta work

and caint git to the bar

But what can Uncle Sam do?

Ain't got no cigarettes

and I ain't got no beer

and ther ain't hardly

any food around here

But what can Uncle Sam do?

The ceilins fallin down

and the pipes er all broke

This ole house ain't nothin

but a joke

But what can Uncle Sam do?

He can bring me back my money

I had in that ole gallon jar

that he took when him and Aunt Lucy

took off and stole my car.

That's what Uncle Sam can do!!

From where?:

I see that a fella from Jersey came down ta spend the
winter in Texas. I guess the other two went ta
Florida!

Far!:

There was a report of a grass far yesterdy about 500
feet off the highway. Yep, it was a grass far alright!
When the far department got there, ther was two
police officers sittin on the hood a ther car smokin a
joint!

Oh Hell:

Darrell never had a real way with women, so when I
took him with me ta this café what had this new

Waitress Angie, that he hadn't met yet, he started right out a flirtin with er!

After he'd made a few wise remarks, Angie said, "Well, let me tell ya, I'd go ta the moon with Wes, I'd go ta Mars with Wes and I'd even go ta Venus with Wes. But, I'm stayin away from yer anus!

Dinner:

I took my family out ta dinner the other night at a nice place. When we went in, an elderly man asked me if I had reservations. I said, "Of course not, if I had any reservations about eatin here I wouldn't a brought my family!"

Oops!:

Darrell's wife got in a fight with a nurse the other day cause when Darrell went in ta the Doctor and told them he had prostate problems, the nurse said she would handle it!

Election?:

A distant cousin from the city came by last week and while I was showin him around the place, he saw the stallion runnin back n forth raisin hell.

Cousin said, "What's wrong with that horse, is he crazy?"

I said, "Nope, he's just all wound up cause he caint make a decision. We got three fillies out there and every one of em's runnin fer mare!"

Wreck:

I really like that song by Carrie Underwood, "Jesus take the Wheel". I especially like the part where the gal is gonna have a wreck and she throws her hands inta the air and says "Jesus take the wheel". My Sister-in-Law done the same thing and I guess the Devil musta been drivin the patrol car she hit!

34

Good call!:

LeRoy went ta a group of specialists cause his arm was hurtin pretty bad and it was crooked. Two doctors came in and looked it over. Then Doctor Burns said, "The problem is your arm has been broke and it has healed wrong. It'll have ta be re-set! Doctor James here will take care of the first part and I'll be right back after the break!"

Darrell's at it again!:

Darrell come runnin in ta my house the other nite and asked if my tractor was runnin real good.
It seems he had made a hundred dollar bet with some city boys that him an me could beat em in a game of Putt Putt Golf!

Pay Who?

I remember when I was a kid, the old folks always said ya had ta "pay the piper". I never knew what they meant til recently. Now I know, it's the people who pump the oil thru them pipelines!!

Patriotism:

I'm right in there when it comes ta doin things
American! Every year when they have "The Great
American Smokeout", I go outside ta do my
smokin!

Bad eatin habits:

My dang ole dog has this bad habit of runnin along
side a car when it goes by and bite'n at the tires! I
guess I cain't blame him tho. I've always got im
watchin tv with me an he's seen too many a them
"meals on wheels" commercials!

Can't Eat?:

My nephew Hollis was lookin fer a house ta rent.
We let him look through our newspaper and after he
had been lookin fer a while he said, "Looky here,
they got a three bedroom trailer here fer rent fer
only $300 a month!" Then he said, "Aw, never
mind, it says No Smokers. Hell if I can't take my
cookin equipment with me I don't want it!"

36.

Jist one!:

Darrell's wife told him she was gonna go down town and buy a parakeet. Darrell got all upset n told her, "Like hell yar, we caint afford no pair a keet, you can only buy one!"

Turnin' 40:

I don't know what it is about women turnin 40 years old, but it seems ta bother em fer some reason. Well, Kuzin Mary jist turned 40 and she was a bawlin and carryin on, sayin she was 40 and didn't never do nothin with er life or nothin. So, Kuzin Earl told er, "Now look Honey, ya done plenty n ya got plenty ta show fer yer life. Ya got me, ya got twelve beautiful kiddos, ya got a nice house trailer." Then he took her ta the back winda and pointed outside n said, "An looky there, ya got yer own line a clothing! Ain't every women yer age can say that!"

Down on the Rio Grande:

I was working down near the Rio Grande in South
Texas a while back. At mid evenin, I saw about fifty
men wading across the Rio Grande tward the United
States and all of em had ponchos on ther shoulders.
Yep, I never seen so many men named Pancho in my
life!

It's a job:

My grandson the other day asked me if he could
spend more time at the library. I said sure, and asked
him why.
He said, "I wanta learn ta be a Bookie!"

Bad news!:

Kids er gittin ta be more trouble all the time! Ther
startin gangs at younger and younger ages.
My cousin Bill told me the other day that his six
month old boy has a "teething ring" already! What's
this world comin too?

38.

Meanwhile back at the border:

I was driving through a small village down there by the border and when I seen people in the streets, I'd beep my horn and wave at em. Well all they did was either give me the bird or shake ther fist at me and I thought, "what an unfriendly bunch a people!"
Then I realized, they wernt unfriendly at all, they jist didn't know how ta wave in English!

Waste of time:

Lately, every time I asked somebody what ther gonna do fer the weekend, they tell me ther gonna jist hang around the house, drink beer an watch the boob tube!
Hell, I can think of a lot more ta do than sit around starin at a womans bra!

No lie:

I was close enough ta listen when this escapee was arrested the other day ta hear what was happnin.
The prisoner said, "I told the Warden that I had

allergies and if I had ta keep eatin that jail food I'd
break out!"

Gittin bigger:
I caint believe how big people think a mattress has ta
be now! They got twin mattresses, then single bed
ones, then doubles, then queens and kings. Now I
heard taday ther havin a "store wide mattress" sale!

How ta git along with yer Redneck neighbor:
Remember that any Road Kill found on the road in
front of his place from property line ta property line
belongs at him!

Don't complain about his trailor not bein skirted.
The breeze underneath keeps the place cooler and
the dogs can git outa the weather a lot easier!

Don't complain about his two holer! If ya want a
higher classed place ta poop, go ta Walmart!

40.

Don't complain bout the cars he's got. He paid good money fer all of em and just cause they don't run don't mean he don't want em! They make damn good storage too!

Leave the door open on the two holer fer at least ten minutes befor ya light a cigarette in there!

When ya use the two holer, use anything but the comic er sports sections. Thems fer readin!

Don't let yer wife pick up an admire that ole brass flower pot next ta the ole mans easy chair! She could make an awful mess!

Ignore them little wiffs a smoke comin' from that other shack, the buildin ain't on fire!

Don't ask what's on the bar-b-que pit, jist eat it!

When yer mowin yer yard, be careful not ta cut the cord running from yer house thru yer line fence!

Don't complain about that raggedy old couch on the porch. If it weren't raggedy it'd be in the house! Would ya want it in yer house?

If ya don't like noise, put up a sound barrier. Hell, it's yer dollar!

And, don't worry about those law boys that's always stoppin in. They always leave with a grin on ther face! Maybe not drivin so well, but shur grinnin!

And don't never complain bout his driveway! Ifn ya don't like muddin, park outside the gate!

Need ta set down some rules:
Darrell came by the other day ta show me a list he'd made up of what a man had ta be ta date his niece, Sally Ann. (Darrell has been raisin' Sally Ann since

42.

the freak accident three years ago when the still blew up n killed er parents. Sally's goin on twelve years old now and needs ta have some set rules.)
Anyway the list was as follers:

The man's gotta have at least a fifth grade edgication. (no less than third grade ifn he's smart)
The man's gotta have at least a part time job.
The man's gotta have a fifties er later model pickup truck.
The man's gotta know huntin' n fishin'.
The man caint be morin fifteen years oldern Sally.

After I read the list Darrell asked me ifn it was okay. I said, "It looks good ta me, cept one thang. The man caint go around braggin all the time jist cause he meets all them there high standards ya set for im! I hate that!

Is this true?!:

I dropped in on Uncle Ed and Aunt Polly the other
day and I guess they was afightin'.

Anyway, I walked in the door jist in time ta hear
Aunt Polly say. "Well ya better jist watch it Ed yer
walkin on thin ice!"

Then Uncle Ed said. "Good! Ya jist admitted I can
walk on water woman, so ya better watch it!"

Women?:

Me and Darrell and a few of our other friends was
sittin at the bar drinkin a few cold beers and talkin
bout the ladies in our lives.

All of a sudden this young scrawny lookin guy come
over ta the table an said. "I got the most beautiful
wife and the most beautiful sister in the world!"

I said. "Oh yeah, got some pictures?"

The boy laid a picture on the table of him and the
most gorgeous bride I'd ever seen and said. "Yep,
that's her right ter with me!"

44.

Cheese?:

Darrell never was much fer shoppin, nor fer listenin neither.

He was havin a Superbowl party this year and when it came time ta go pick up the beer his wife said, "when yer gitten yer beer, pick me up some Parmesan cheese."

Well, Darrell was gone fer quite a while and when he got back he walked in the door and said, "Now woman before ya say anything, I didn't fergit! I went ta every store in town, includin them there conveenyence stores and nobody had any Farmer John Cheese!"

Oh I see:

I was drivin down Slaughter Lane in Austin, Texas the other day and had just mentioned how long it was takin ta git the constuction done along there, when we came upon a sign that said, "Slow construction entrance ahead!"

Counterfeit!:

Darrell said he took his truck in fer repairs the other
day and they slapped him with a two hundred eighty
six dollar bill!

I said, "Wow Darrell, that's unreal!"

Still lookin:

I met up with Jimmy Joe at the bar the other day. I
hadn't seen him since he moved north about three
years ago.

We got ta talkin bout this n' that and I asked him.

"So Jimmy Joe, it's been a long time! What brings
ya back down this way?"

"Awe", said Jimmy Joe, "I'm lookin fer a new dish
washer, mine went out about a month ago and she
never came back!"

Show some respect!:

My grandson goes to a small school of only about
two hundred students.

They had a school assembly with an important

46.

Historian as speaker. The speaker started talking about history and about our forefathers. When he started the part about our forefathers, my grandson got up real quick and yelled, "Hey asswhole, just cuz we's all rednecks here, don't mean we don't have morn' four fathers amongst us!"

What is it with drugs?
They tell ya ta take aspirin so's ya don't git blood clots what cause a stroke. But if ya have a blood clotting disorder, don't take aspirin!

Ya go ta git an allergy drug ta clear ya up so's ya can breath and it's says, "this drug may cause upper respiratory infection" or "don't take this drug if you have excess mucus!"

Ya go and git ya a sleep aide and it says "caution: may cause drowsiness!"

I hear the Government is willin ta pay thousands of dollars to anyone who can come up with a drug ta make people stop takin drugs!

The United States Navy is considerin banning prescription drugs cause so many of em say, "this product may lead to a decrease in seaman!"

Some people are heartless:
The local zoo got rid of Waldo the seal the other day. They said it was cuz he wouldn't play with his balls fer the people anymore!

That don't work:
Women always reserve the right ta change ther minds.
The other day Arlie's wife threw him out of an airplane then yelled down at im, "Honey, I'm sorry. I love ya. Please come back!"

48.

Mis-understanding:

Darrell told me that fer the last two weeks, every time he walks in the house he gits one hell of a tounge lashin'.

I said. "What the hell'd ya do Darrell?"

"Nothin" Darrell said, "the bitch lost all her pups and all she wants now is attention!"

In the news:

I seen in the news the other night that there is something in the rine of watermelon that acts like Viagra when a man eats it!

That explains a lot since Hope, Arkansas which is the watermelon capital of the nation, is also the Home Town of President Bill Clinton!

There was a statement made that a good percentage of men in the United States prefer women who were born abroad! I am one of those men, cuz I sure as hell wouldn't want one who was born a man!

The energy crisis:

I think the problem with the oil crisis throughout the world is probably good for the marriage, cuz politicians is now beginnin to encourage more drilling at home!

Speakin of relatives:

Darrell told me last night that he had been half-mooned by one of his in-laws yesterday! I can understand what he was sayin', cuz I just put in a half bath myself!

A little poetry:

Followin are a couple poems I writ in the year 2007
I was up til almost midnight er maybe have past eleven.
The first one tells of a party and tells quite a tail
Where everybody got in a fight, but nobody went ta jail.
The second tells a story that really ain't no joke
It's about the hard times and how I'm goin broke.

50.

A Redneck New Years Eve:

Twas the night before new years
and down on the farm,
we were havin a party
an never meant no harm.

There was bar-b-que, liquor 'n
beer of all kinds
an fer sissy men 'n ladies
there was two dollar wines.

The brisket 'n beans was
so doggone good,
I woulda ate it all
if I could!

There was dancing 'n singin
'n a couple poker games.
Ther was so many people
I didn't know all ther names!

It started gittin drunk out
at about dark thirty
'n some a the folks was
agittin quite flirty!

The party went on 'n
inta the night.
Then Larry 'n Bob got
into a fight!

51.

Larry socked Bob
knocked im right over the table,
right inta the lap
of Orville's wife Mable!

Mable slapped Bob 'n
Bob smacked Larry
'n knocked im inta a gal
named Mary!

Mary slapped Billy
n' Billy smacked Jake,
n' I heard him yell
"Hey gimme a break!"

Jake picked up Billy
like a big ole he-man,
n' spun im around 'n
throwed im in the trash can!

Then one a the women
clum Jakes back.
'n coverd Jakes head with
a big ole tote sack!

Another one kicked
ole Jake in the ass,
'n he went a rollin
inta the grass!

52.

He rolled over 'n over
like he was on fire
'n slammed right
inta the tractor tire!

Jake started laughin'
from inside the sack
'n Larry retched over 'n
slapped Bob on the back!

Larry said, "Let's have a beer
ya ole son-of-a-gun!"
'n Bob said, "I cain't remember
when I've had so much fun!

Then all of a sudden
at the stroke of midnight,
a big ole flash
lit up the nite.

Then right behind it there
came a loud pop,
n' all the rabbits in ther cages
started ta hop!

The cats 'n the dogs
scurried under the hay
'n then my ass
started ta bray!

More booms, bangs 'n flashes
lit up the night
'n all the hogs started
ta take flight!

They tore down the fence 'n
ran out in the yard
I said, "now catchin them things
is gonna be hard!

Then all of a sudden
the stud started kickin.
I said, "I don't think my gates
C'n take such a lickin!

Everybody was gone by dawn
'n ther weren't no one around
but ther was bottles, cans, papers
'n beer kegs scattered all over the ground!

Ther weren't no animals anywhere,
at least that I could see!
So I sat down 'n popped open a beer
'n said, "Why does this happen ta me?!"

I spent two days at findin stock
'n fixin up the farm.
But hey, I still don't think a little party
will ever do no harm!

54.

Goin Broke!
I'm sixty two years old
damn near sixty three,
an I cain't hardly make it
on Social Security!

I get my check each month an by the time I pay the
rent
an git all my necessities the whole damn check is
spent!

I cain't git no extras
like clothes ta cover my hide.
Hell, I'm lucky I got a pair a shoes
that's even fit ta be tied!

The house is fallin around me
in total dis-repair.
An I cain't even buy shampoo
ta wash my nasty hair!

The truck won't start most a the time,
so it's sittin in the grass.
an even if it did start,
I couldn't afford no gas!

The front gates fallen off an
won't hardly open.
An I'll tell ya right now friend,I'm havin trouble
copen!

The neighbor came by
an started his braggin.
An told me I could git a job
if I'd just go on the wagon!

So I set out on the wagon
fer two days drinkin beer.
An dreamin bout my fishin
an goin out an huntin deer!

After all that time a waitin
nobody came an give me a job.
So I went over by the line fence
an stood an laughed at Bob!

I've been tryin ta think a things
ta make things a little better.
Especially since the government
sent me a nasty letter!

I guess I could win the lottery
or maybe I'll write a book.
An maybe I can make enough
ta git me off the hook!
But right now Folks, I'm Goin Broke!

56.

What's the problem?

I decided ta make some extra money, so I put an ad
in the local paper statin' that I'd teach people ta do
the shuffle fer only $50. The people signed up and
sent ther money to me in advance.
Come the day of the lessons ther shur was a lot of
pissed off people when I handed each of em a deck
of cards as they came thru the door!

What a dumb judge!

Uncle Cooter had ta go ta court fer his drinkin cause
he'd been arrested fer Public Intoxication just too
many times.
Well, the judge told Cooter he wasn't gonna put im
in jail, but was givin him a 30 days suspended
sentence and he had ta join the 12 step program.
When Cooter came home, he said. "What a dumb
judge, don't he realize that the more I dance, the
more I wanna drink?"

Home Schoolin:

Maw and me took our grandkids outa public school
ta home school em cause the public school was
teachin em ta be hit men!
Every day when they came home from school they'd
hit us up fer another twenty bucks!

Another sign:

I was drivin in ta Austin ta take Maw ta work the
other day and ther was a sign along the road that
said, "Lady Lions basketball rocks"!
What ta hell are basketball rocks?

Beautiful:

We put an ad in the paper ta sell our mare.
Yesterday, a guy and his wife come by ta look at er.
The lady started pettin the horse and sayin how
pretty the horse was.
I said. "Ya think she's pretty now, wait til ya see her
bridal pictures!"

I told im!:

I got home from work taday and set down ta supper
right away, as usual.
About the time I got my plate filled, maw said.
"Well, Cooter got his house leveled taday."
I said. "I told Cooter that would happen if'n he
didn't operate that stil outside where it was safe!"

Glasses?

Bubba got stopped by the cops the other day and he
had a glass of beer in each hand! When the officer
asked what he was doin, Bubba said. "Them folks
down there at the license place told me I had ta drive

with glasses. I figured I might as well have somthin
in em! Good idea huh?"
SUPRIZE! Bubba got arrested.

Incognito:

I stopped by Darrell's the other day ta git im ta go
with me ta git some fly masks fer my horses.
When I told Darrell what I was goin for he said.
"Okay, but two questions. How ya gonna git the
masks on the flies and what makes ya think the
horses won't still reconize em?"

The Line:

My grandson and me went inta town the other night
ta git some stuff Maw wanted.
When we got inta town, there was people lined up
on the sidewalks fer several blocks! Some of em
standin, some sittin and some of even layin down
with ther heads on back packs.
My grandson asked. "Hey Papa, who are all those
people and what er they doin?"
I said. "Them's wait watchers son. Ther a buncha
movie geeks that stand in line and wait fer hours er
even days ta watch every new movie that comes ta
town!"

Redneckly Correct:

Politician: A person running for political office.
Redneckly correct: A Damned Liar!

Petition: A flyer sent around for people signatures to get something brought before the proper channels for voting, etc.
Redneckly correct: a wall in the barn seperatin a couple stalls or tack rooms.

Arrested subject: A person taken into custody for an infraction of law.
Redneckly correct: A fellar who has had plentya rest.

Doctor: A person licensed to tend to the medical needs of another.
Redneckly correct: Held back part of her pay!

Discussing: Talking something over.
Redneckly correct: saying yer sorry fer cussin'.

Lawyer: A person licensed to represent another in a court action.
Redneckly correct: Another Damned Liar!

Feedback: A response to information received.
Redneckly correct: when ya don't need no more

feed, ya put the feed back!

Lightning: A flash of light in the sky caused by electricity.
Redneckly correct: (spelled lightning') an alcoholic drink, what can make ya go blind if'n ya drink too much of it!

Newspaper: A written compilation of daily or weekly news from around the country.
Redneckly correct: Paper what ya use in the two holer fer cleanup.

Comics: A compilation of sketches and written communications intended for amusement.
Redneckly correct: The part of the paper ya read when yer in the two holer. (check out the political section too. It's even funnier!).

Outdated: Old or obsolete.
Redneckly correct: a fellar what got less dates than his buddy!

Full moon: when you can see the moon as an entire circle.
Redneckly correct: pants down, shirt up with yer whole ass showin'!

Crash test: A test the government insists on to make sure cars are safe in case of a wreck.
Redneckly correct: sneekin out ta the truck ta see how much sleep you can git for ya git caught.

Crash test dummie: An adult sized doll used during a crash test.
Redneckly correct: a person who thinks they kin sneek out ta the truck and git some shuteye when Maw's around!

Shot record: A medical record of a persons immunizations.
Redneckly correct: a record of how many shots ya far'd from yer gun.

Post par-tum depression: An illness a woman gets after giving birth to a child.
Redneckly correct: what yer doctor sees when he tells ya ta bend over and spread yer cheeks.

Delivery: taking something to someone.
Redneckly correct: A place where de horses is kept.

62.

<u>Postage:</u> The cost involved in sending mail.
Redneckly correct: The age of them ole fence posts.

<u>Decided:</u> Made a decision.
Redneckly correct: took the side off of. (that thar tree decided mah truck).

<u>Identical:</u> Exactly alike.
Redneckly correct: the place in yer head where yer eyeball goes.

<u>Surrounded:</u> being boxed in from all sides.
Redneckly correct: a very fat officer.

<u>Abroad:</u> over seas
Redneckly correct: a female.

<u>Shut up:</u> be quiet!
Redneckly correct: Woman, git 'n the truck!

<u>Aboard:</u> on top of, riding on, as on board a bus.
Redneckly correct: a piece of lumber used fer construction purposes.

Pushin a product?

I see that there are a lot of clothing optional cafés
around the country now!
I'd say it's cause ther just tryin ta push the Strip
Steak!

That Darrell!

Yeah, ole Darrell has turned inta a regular strip
tease!
He holds twenty dollar bills up til the stripper gits
close enough, then puts a dollar in ther bra!

What'd they say?

Aint Ella has been makin money fer quite a few
years as a seamstress, makin dresses n such.
Well, the other day my little granddaughter came up
ta me an asked, "Papa, how can Aint Ella make any
money makin dresses?"
"Well, I said, she makes em an sells em ta other
women."
"That's what I thought", she said "but I heard em
say on TV that ya should rip what ya sew!"

64.

Who's Comin?

Hanks daughter was in the third grade and wasn't
doin to well in her classes. So, the teacher told her
she was gonna send a tutor over ta see her folks one
evenin after school..
Well the girl came home from school all excited n
went up ta Hank and said, "Paw, ya better git ready,
cause the teacher is sendin a tooter over here and
he's probly gonna raise an awful stink!"

Who's the boss:

I caint fer the life a me figger why a woman'll say
she rules the house and when ya git inside ther's a
sign on the wall that says "House Rules"

Gas Prices:

Lately with the gas prices the way they been , some
of the politicians are tryin ta say thers a shortage a
gas!
Well, I tell ya what, these guys ain't been to a good
Redneck beer party er walked passed Uncle Jesse's
two holers lately if'n they think thers a gas shortage!

Barak Obama says that if'n ya wanna save on gas
and keep from havin ta drill fer oil here in these here
United States, all ya gotta do is properly inflate yer
tires an git a tuneup!
Well, I think thers a couple a local gas stations in my
town here that's backin the big oil companies, cause
I went ta fill up my tires with air an ther air pumps
didn't work! Reckon I'll have ta sue em! And, that
there tuneup..Well, I had ta git an appointment, so
that waitin'll probly cost me a fortune in gas too!!

Know where yar:

My granddaughter decided ta go stay with some
friends in England and tour Europe!
I told her she needed ta be shur of where she was,
cause I went ta China ta stay with some friends and
ended up stayin with the wong family!

Screens:

For some reason, a man can go thru the process of
puttin a screen door on the house ta keep out bugs.
Right? Then every time his wife wants ta holler
something out the door, she'll open the screen!
Kinda defeats the purpose. Don't it? Lessen they jist
don't wanna strain ther voices!

66.

Women say the damndest thangs:

I went over ta see Darrell the other day and he was
workin on a couple of his trailers. He was tryin ta
build new tounges on em, so I started helpin im.
Next thing I knew, his wife was yellin out the screen
door. (she opened it first of course) And she said.
"Honey, Dave from down at the hardware called and
said he has two inch balls and will hold on to em til
you can git down there and pick em up!

Family Vacations:

Usually when ya go on a family vacation yer in a
hurry ta git ta yer destination. Right?
Well, you should teach yer family how to make it
easier ta git there on time.
The main thing they need ta learn is: Ta keep from
wastin time, they need ta time ther waste!

My Dad wasn't much fer swearin:

At least not around us kids!
One day my little brother and me went ta help Dad
tear down an old house fer the materials.
Well, Dad always done it clean. We'd take a few
boards off, then we'd have ta pull the nails out of em
before we tore any more down.
Dad gave me a big crowbar and while he held the

two by four between his knees, he had me start
pullin the nails. Well, one nail in peticular was given me some
problems, so I give it all I had and yanked that
sucker. All of a sudden Dad's end a the two by four
raised up an hit im (you know where) and Dad
jumped about three feet in the air and yelled, "Son of
a Bitch!"
I tried ta apologize, but it was so funny watchin him
and seein the look on my little brothers face fore he
started laughin, that I couldn't do nothin but laugh!
After a few minutes and doin some more work, Dad
started laughin too! So, all in all, except the shock of
him swearin in front of us, I guess everthing was
okay!

Mom didn't either but, Surprise!

Mom was usually a patient woman, but on this
peticular night she was tired an just wanted ta go
home.
We had been to one of her friends house all day and
as we pulled out of the driveway headed fer home,
the old local pain in the ass was walkin down the
middle of the road with a wheelbarrel full a fire
wood. He stayed right in the road, just a walkin slow
and when we'd try ta pass, he'd swerve out just
enough ta keep us from passin.
Mom finally had enough and she layed on the horn.
The old man jumped up in the air and threw his

68.

Hands in the air, throwing the wheelbarrel fer a flip
and dumpin the wood all over the road.
It was so funny that all us kids just busted out
laughin!
Then Mom maneuvered the car around him and
yelled, "You Horses Ass!"
All of a sudden there was shock and awe throughout
the car and then laughter again. Now we was
laughin at Mom cause all we usually heard her say
was "oh pooh!"
I guess we shouldn't a been that surprised tho cuz
mom was kinda a wild lady. Hell every New Years
Eve she'd drink a whole 6oz. gin highball and smoke
a cigarette!

Banking:

I think the way that banks are goin down lately and
bein picked up by the FDIC, somebody aughta buy
up these banks and call ther company, "Amnesty
Banking Services!" Let me know what ya think!

He just don't get it:

When I was younger, I was at my Grampas house when a man pulled in with a fancy sports car and asked ta talk ta grampa.
I didn't go outside, as ya didn't never go out n git involved in grampa's conversations if'n ya knew what was good fer ya!
Anyway, after the man n grampa talked a while, the man left and grampa came inside laughin".
Gramma said, "what's so funny paw?"
Grampa said, "That there man was a lookin fer a place fer some kids ta drag race. Said he heard we had 160 acres a open field back there and wanted ta let em drag race back there. Said he'd pay me five hundred bucks an I could charge people five bucks a piece ta watch em drag!
Doggone if that don't beat all, me gittin my fields done and them a payin ME fer it too!"

What a doc!:

I was havin troubles with my ears a while back. So, I called the doctor and told im I had this ringin in my ears.
"Did it stop when I answered the phone?" he asked.
I said, "yeah it did".
The doc said, "that'll be fifty bucks, I'll send ya the bill" and he hung up!

70.

A lesson learned:

When I was in the eighth grade, we had a class on lessons learned, where the teacher had students stand up and tell about somethin they or somebody else did that they learned a lesson from.
Well Bubba stood up and told us about how he'd got caught by his daddy smokin out behind the barn and how daddy made im smoke ten cigarettes, one right after tother.
When he finished his story, the teacher asked, "Did ya learn yer lesson here?"
Bubba said, "I sure did, next time I'm gonna make sure daddy catches me with a girl back there!"

Great mileage:

My grandson the other day got 400 miles on a gallon of gas!
Yeah, we didn't realize it til we got there and found he had been sittin on a blanket with the gas can under it in the back seat!

Chupacabra:

I've been hearin so much on the news all over the country about the wild beast called the chupacabra, that I don't mind tellin ya, I'm skeerd!

Yep, it's probly gonna take me some time ta git over bein skeerd a this thang, so my wife may have ta do all the chores n take out the trash fer a while!

Oh no they don't:

I was watchin one a them infomercials on tv the other day and they made a good long speil about ther product and then said.
"The first one hundred people that call with yer credit card will git free shippin and a bonus!"
I said. "Are they talkin ta me? Ther better not be a hundred people callin with my credit card!"

Can ya tell me this?

Why is it that the girl who wears a shirt that says "I'm Hot" on the front and wears pants that say "Try Me" on the ass of em are the first ones ta holler about sexual harrassment?

Not to insult anyone:

But, I heard tell that the favorite dish of a cannibal is "Battered Wives"!

72.

Last Call:

Lester told me the other day that he always stays at
the bar til "last call".
Yep, he say's his wife calls and calls while he's
there, but waits fer her ta say, "This is my last call, if
ya don't git yer ass home, I'm comin down there'!

A real money maker:

Many years back, the country outlawed the "out
house".
Well, my two uncles, (bein the rednecks they is)
decided this wasn't so bad after all.
They got ther trucks and trailers and went around
the country pickin up the old "out houses" fer
nothing just so's people could git rid of em. Then
they brought em back to my uncle's farm and got
some green paint and painted em up, got some
lumber and put legs on some of em. They dedicated
an acre of land for the purpose and set all of em up
on that acre and sold em fer fishin shanties and deer
blinds!
I'll tell ya what, the local sporting goods shops got
pretty dog gone mad but my uncles made a killin!

Good dog:

Darrell had this ole coon dog he called Ole Blue.
That dog was the best dog I've ever seen fer playin
dead!
Darrell and him would go out huntin for hours and
when they got home, Darrell and Ole Blue would sit
down and share a few beers. After drinkin those
beers, Darrell would say, "All right, that's it Blue,
play dead."
Ole Blue would lay down on his side with his legs
and tail stretched out straight and he'd whine a
couple times, let a good one rip and lay still.
Yep, he was the best there was. He not only looked
dead, he smelled dead too!

Dad was good at this:

When I was younger, I was tryin to help my dad
build a shed out by the barn. My little four year old
cousin kept on bothering me, wantin to help. I
couldn't get him to leave me alone, so finally I told
him to go ask his uncle (my dad) if he could help
him.
He went over to dad and said, " Wes said you would
let me help."
My dad looked at him and said, "Well you sure can.
These boards are too long. Go tell yer aunt I need a
can of shortening."
I was surprised to see him run off to tell mom.

74.

I said, "Wow, that worked, but he won't be gone long."
Dad said, "When he comes back, just tell him it was the wrong kind!"

Since this is election year, I decided ta write
down some of the political agenda according to
Rednecks! I asked around and talked to a lot of
Rednecks so I could give you the real stuff! So,
this is what the majority said. Majority rules.
Right?

On Immigration:
They use the words of The Oakridge Boys, "You
don't have ta go home but ya can't stay here!"

On Racial Discrimination:
"If you don't like Nascar, ya don't belong in these
here United States!"

Our Policy in times of War:
"Grab a cold tater and wait. When they start across
our borders Git yer gun and Git er done!"

Foreign Policy:
"Every foreigner should have a life insurance policy.
If they give us any crap they'll need it!"

Energy Independence:
"We had the energy ta gain our independence, now
we can use our independence ta gain energy!"

Environment:
"Take care of the farm and the farm'll take care of
you!"

Social Security:
"Nobody gits it but them what worked fer it! The Government and them that didn't work fer it can dip ther own snuff!"

Education:
"Home schoolin's the best. Some book learnin, some in the wood shed and some out behind the barn! A dad burn public school ain't got all that!"

Space program:
"Give everbody plenty a space and we'll all git along!"

Special Interests:
"Wimmin, beer, bar-b-que, rodeo, football and Nascar!"

Gun Laws:
"Refer ta pages 25 and 26."

Health care:
"No national health care plan. Ya don't never let the government know yer sick er they'll put ya on the deceased list and ya lose yer Social Security!

Well, that's about it fer now, when we come up with some more we'll shur let ya know!

What is he dumb er what?

I had my little spare pickup truck fer sale and this
guy came by ta look at it.
He looked it over good and said, "Ya got a Title fer
that truck?"
I said, "Yeah, it's a Ford Ranger!"

What's the problem?

My Uncle Bill is just a plain ole redneck lawyer and
he was defendin this guy who was charged with
drunk drivin.
Well, Uncle Bill nor the man he was defendin felt
like appearin in court on Oct. 1st, so Uncle Bill sent a
letter to the judge. The letter stated that the man
could not appear for a Hearing because the man was
deaf!
Uncle Bill was held in contempt of court and the
man was charged fer failure to appear! Now ain't
That a bitch?

Hold it:

Ya know, I used ta be able ta pass gas in my old
pickup truck. Now the cost of that is so high I have
ta stop at every station!

78.

A little laundry advice:
If yer prone ta gas and ya wear long tailed shirts,
either leave em untucked or be shur and wear
underwear. The Ole Lady says gittin them skid
marks outa shirt tales is a bitch!

Media:

Have ya noticed how the media gits involved in
everything and then just keeps it going?
There has been a lot of talk in the last few years
about drugs in sports and they have been hitting
teams like Dallas Cowboys exta hard. I mean,
comeon. Every time the Cowboys ask for a time out
in a game the announcer says "Dallas is gonna burn
one now!"

The Poor Guys:

I don't know where I get the idea that the boys from
CBS don't have the best marriages, but I do know
that they are the only ones who have "Desperate
Housewives."

Can't tell:

When I was younger I always wanted to be a Secret
Service Agent.
Sorry, I can't tell ya if I ever did, cause that would
be releasing government secrets!

Old jobs, modern names:

As ya'll know, in recent years, they have come up
with sophisticated names fer old jobs. Such as, a
Housewife is now a Domestic Specialist or a
Housekeeper is a Household Maintenance
Technician and so on.
Well, the other day, we were sittin, watchin Tv after
supper when my grandson started passin gas over
and over again! Well, finally my wife looked at him
and said, "You are a regular little stinker now.
Aren't ya?"
Little Billy looked at her and said, "No Grandma.
I'm a Fart Fabrication Specialist!"

More damn taxes:

I heard just the other day that the NAP (National
Association of Pimps) wants to levy an
entertainment tax on anyone who has a Big Country
Hodown!

80.

Kids like excitement even if ther ain't none:

The other day, Bubba came over ta pick up his
trailer that he had lent me a while back.
I lifted the tung of the trailer whilst he was backin up
ta hitch it to his truck.
As he was backin up, I hollered to him, "Slow down
now. Yer gonna hit me!"
Then when he got close enough I hollered, "Whoa
stop!"
Then I hollered at him and said, "Okay, I'm gonna
jump on yer tounge."
Next thing I knew, here come all the grandkids a
runnin down the hill, Billy in the lead, hollerin
"Come on everybody ther's gonna be a fight!"

My opinion:

Lately, there has been a huge increase in the number
of Redneck beer parties where Law Enforcement
personel have been confiscating kegs of beer.
It is my opinion, that they should bring the draft
back!

What about us?

The inmates in the Texas Prison System are upset.
They want to know why they can't have the "Cell
Free Zones" like they are establishing for school
districts and other places around the country!

OU-Texas Football game:

My friend Cody (who lives in town) decided ta have
a party for the game and asked me ta bring my
famous "Atomic Bomb Chili".
Cody bought a keg of beer for the occasion.
There were ten of us all together and we started
right in on the keg while we waited for game time.
At the end of the first quarter (score OU 7-Texas 3)
we were all startin ta git hungry, so we all had a
bowl of chili.
I ate my chile then asked Hank ta roll me a cigarette.
Hank took one out of his pack and rolled it across
the coffee table to me and said, "Better make this
yer last one cause it's gonna git gassy in here purty
soon.
At half time (score OU 21 Texas 20) we ate us some
more chili. By the time half time was over, ole Hank
was startin ta git edgy and after five minutes into the
second half, I heard Hank say, "Oh Lordy" and he
let out a rumble that smelled like somebody had
died!
It wasn't long before Darrell, Earle, Bubba and

82.

Cody started tootin in unison! Then me and the others joined in and by the end of the 3rd quarter (score OU 28 Texas 30) Everybody was rootin and tootin and fartin and dartin and havin a great ole time til the whole place was just plain foggy and rank!

Needless ta say, we didn't git ta see the last quarter cause just as it started we heard sirens outside and all kind a noise. When we looked outside and there was firetrucks, the police and the epa with their air quality machine sittin out there! The people were all wearin gas masks and they were evacuatin the neighbors from their homes!

Well, this was exciting, so we all ran outside ta see what was goin on.

They made us get down the street and then barged inta Cody's house with hoses and detectors of some kind and everything else! They tore the place up lookin fer what they told us later they thought might be a gas leak!

Well ta make a long story short, when they found out what was really goin on, we were arrested fer disorderly conduct fer causin noxious odors in a public place!

We ended up payin $200 each in fines and the following day the City Council passed an ordinance against possession of my chili within the city limits! And people try ta tell me gas is gittin cheaper!

By the way, the final score fer the OU-Texas game was OU 35 texas 45! Go Longhorns! And, Darrell says the next time maybe we should have a few boiled eggs ta keep the chili settled down!

Darrell is shoppin again!

It was gittin toward the end of the month and the end of the money fer Darrell and his wife, so she told him ta go ta town and pick up some Vermicelli. Well, as usual Darrell was gone fer quite some time and when he came back, he walked in and threw some road kill on the table and said, "Well, here's the fixins Mama. Them stores didn't have no Vermin Chili, so you'll have ta make yer own!

Quite a compliment, I thought:

Went over ta see Darrell the other day and when I got there his wife told me he was out back changin the oil on the old ford.
I went out back and just as I got out there, Darrell came out from under the truck just a spittin and sputterin, with oil all over his face and all down the front of him. Somehow he had been directly under the oil pan when he took out the plug.
I got a good laugh at him, but I did go and git him a shop towel ta wife off with AFTER I told him how good he looked in HD!

84.

That really ticks me off!!

I didn't git a chance ta watch Nascar Races last week, but I thought, "oh well, they said ther gonna have the race results on tv.
Wouldn't ya know it, their race results was about nothin but the Presidential Election!

Government Studies show:

During times such as hurricanes, tornadoes or other inclement weather people find it hard to hold on to their property! ....Who'd figure?

Fifty percent of all married heterosexuals are men! Yeah right, and I'll bet the rest are women!

The earlier a person leaves for their destination, the better the chance of them getting there on time!........ Damn their good!

The best way a woman can prevent pregnancy is to just not have sex! ....Ya Reckon?

If the auto makers build cars that get better gas mileage, the nation will use less gas!

As more and more people are getting older and needing medical attention, the nations medical costs are on the rise!

Now that's scarey:

I was standing out in the back yard when I heard a
voice say, "I wanna be a vet!"
I looked around and all I could see was my little ole
Chevy Nova sittin there!
Boy, was I glad ta see the kids come out from the
other side of the storage building!

Change:

Barak Obama, during his run fer the Presidency
stated he'd like ta change our National Anthem to
"I'd like to teach the world to sing"!
Well, when the Mexican President heard that he
said, "Si, and we would like to change ours to
'Don't fence me in'!"

What ta?

The Grandkids wanted ta go swimmin the other day
at the pool rather than the creek.
When we got there, there was a sign that said, "No
Swimming, pool table is low"!

Poor kid:

My youngest grandson came to me the other day
with his duck. It had been mauled by the dog and the

86.

poor kid was cryin his eyes out!
He settled down when I told him, "It'll be okay son,
we'll get it taken care of. One thing ther ain't no
shortage of around these parts is Quack Doctors!

A minor purchase:

My friend Darrell and I went golfing the other day
and when we went in the Pro-Shop, my brother
asked for some golf tees.

The man acted like a used car salesman!

The man picked up a couple of tees and said, "These
are the best thing you'll ever get to rest your balls
on while waiting to drive.

If you'll look at the seat here on
these tees, you'll see that they have just the right cup
size so that your balls won't be blown off during a
practice swing and you can see how smooth the
surface is. This
makes it very easy to drive without
scratching your balls.

Yes sir, hitting your balls from these tees will really
make them soar.

I also have some balls here that have never
been hit, scratched or played with!"

Darrell told him, "I'll take two bags of the tees, but I ain't gonna bite on those balls!"

For my own safety:

My wife likes to kick around in her sleep at night and is always thrashing until she pushes me right off of the bed.

So, I put a twin sized mattress on the floor on my side of the bed with a three sided tent on it and faced the opening toward the bed.

I call it my fallout shelter!

Laundry?

I stopped by to ask Darrell to go with me to the wash house.
Darrell asked me why the hell I would want him to go to the wash house with me.

I said, "I got a chance to play in a washer pitchin contest and I need somebody to practice with!"

88.
Fence Posts:

Darrell went to the new feed store in town and
bought some fence posts.

Boy was he mad, he ordered eight foot steel posts
and they delivered six footers.

When I went over to see him, he was just a rantin
about those posts.

I said, "Hell Darrell, I'd just load up them posts and
go back down there and demand
to talk to their Postmaster!"

My three dogs:

About a year ago, I bought three worthless old
Coon Dogs from Darrell.

No matter what command ya gave em, Ben
would stand still, George would crouch down and
Joe would lay down and roll over!

I took em to a trainer and the trainer supposedly
trained em!

When I got em back, Ben would still stand still,
George would crouch down and Joe would lay
down and roll over.

So, because I got to lovin the old dogs, I just kep
em and renamed em "Stop, Drop and Roll!"

Fixin up my bar:

Darrell and his wife came over to visit and my wife
wasn't home.

When his wife asked me where my wife was I said,
"Well, you know how big this living room is, well I
told my wife I wanted to put a bar in one end of it
and she told me that was fine, but she got to pick
out the décor because she wanted it to look nice. I
said that was fine with me.
So her and her sister are down town now
looking at stool samples."

Fishin:

Darrell and I went fishing the other day and neither
one of us had any license.
We caught a whole bunch of huge fish though.

When we got through, I threw the stringer full of
fish in the back of the truck, but didn't pay any
attention to the fact the tailgate was left open.

90.

So, as we were driving down the road, the fish started floppin and slid out the tail gate. The stringer got caught though and let the fish drag behind the truck, bouncing all
over the road.

We got stopped by the Game Warden and he asked to see our fishin licenses.

When I got out, I could see the skinned up fish layin behind the truck.

When we said we had no fishin licenses, the Game Warden said he would have to arrest us for fishing without a license and possession of the fish!

Then I told the Game Warden,
"We didn't catch them fish officer, them's road kill and we was draggin em home fer the cats!"

At the wedding:

Ma and me went to my Nieces wedding and it was just as purty as two speckled puppies! The reception was even better.

They had the barn all decorated up real purty and the floor was all shined up fer dancin. They had colored lights turnin all around in the top of
the barn.

Then a guy came in with this bubble machine and made bubbles, big bubbles that floated all over the place.

My niece said they were so beautiful with all the colors that she wish she could keep em all!

So, I asked her why she don't go ahead and keep em.

She said, "how am I supposed to do that?"
I said, "Ain't you never heard of bubble wrap??!"

What a dream:

I went ta bed real late the other night and I started havin bad dreams right off!

I dreamed that I died and went ta Hell and a whole bunch of the girls from my school days were there!
I guess that proves that all dogs don't go ta Heaven!

The Sale:

This Spring, I decided ta take my old milk cow in ta the sale.
She was pretty old and wasn't producin much milk anymore and cost more ta keep than I thought she was worth.

92.

Well, come sale day, Ole Charlie Cannon was there
as usual, struttin his stuff around the sale barns.

Charlie is a rich rancher in the area that has more
money and more ego than he knows what ta do
with.

Charlie drives a big ole Cadillac car with longhorns
on the hood and dresses in a white
suit and wears a big ole white
cowboy hat. He always has an un-lit ceegar
hangin out of his mouth.

There ain't a rancher or farmer in the county or in
several counties fer that matter that don't hate the
man.

Charlie comes in every sale day and has ta strutt
around the barns and make sure he is seen and that
he sees every head of livestock there! He won't just
look over the
herd, he's gotta git down there with em and see
all of em up close.

Well, this day he was standin behind my old cow,
braggin ta another rancher about this n that and
makin fun of my ole cow.

Well, my ole cow had just come off of fresh spring
grass.

She all of a sudden let out a big ole cough and when
she did, it came out her backside like a bullet. Nice
spring green color and got ole Charlie from head ta
foot! It was
even drippin off poor ole Charlies ceegar!

Ya could hear ole Charlie cussin fer half
a mile.

Come time fer the sale, the story had gotten
around ta every farmer and rancher that was there
and some that wasn't, and that ole cow brought me
twice as much from the sale than the best cow there!

The man who bought er, Bob Hanes, put er in his
barn and says he won't part with that sweet ole cow
fer any amount a money!

Damned tack shops!:

I was ridin the horse the other day along a country
road near home and I ran into a car!

Thankfully, me and the horse weren't hurt, but it
done a lot a damage ta the car.
Well the man called the police, cause he was
mad and wanted a report on the accident!

The officer asked me what happened and I said,
"Well, I was ridin my horse down the road and had

just gotten her inta a gallop when he pulled out of
that side road in front of me.
I guess he didn't see me and I know he couldn't hear
me cause he had his windas up and my saddle horn
didn't work!"

Contests:

Darrell and me went ta the County Fair and we had
a great time while we was there. We even entered
some contests!

Well Darrell won the dance contest, the cow chip
pitchin contest and the chicken pluckin contest!

He shouldn't a won the chicken pluckin contest, but
he had been chokin his chicken all day long, so it
was real limp and easy ta pluck!

Wrong Doc:

Darrell's old coon hounds kept gittin sick on him
and no matter how many times he took em ta the
Vet, they just didn't seem ta git any better!

Finally, I told Darrell, "Ya need ta take them dogs ta
somebody that knows somethin about hound dogs,
not no damn Lab Tech!"

Another Mis-understanding:

I needed a new electrical switch last week, so I went to one of those big discount stores.

When I walked into the store, a nice looking young lady came straight up to me and asked,

"Can I help you with something?"

I said, "Yeah, how about a three way switch?"

After I picked myself up off the floor, I asked her nicely where the hardware department was!

Cell Phones?

Friends, don't git yerself one of them cell phones unless yer ready fer trouble!

I went over ta Darrell's the other day and I called home and I left this message while I was driving.

"Hi Honey, I'm over at Darrell's. His wife's not home so we're gonna play some poker. I'll be home for supper and hope ya make one a yer great cakes fer dessert! Love ya sweet thang!"

96.

When I got home, as soon as I walked in the door I
was met with a smack in the back a the head and
two great big kicks in the crotch!

I said, "Hey woman, what the hell's up?"
She said, "Don't ask me what's up!"

Then she turned on the answering machine and this
is my message that was there!:
"Hi Honey, I'm over at Darrell's wife's. Gonna
poker. I'll be home fer dessert! Ya thang!"

Farm Equipment?

Young Elmo got himself a three point hitch from ole
Lester Barker the other day!

Yeah, Lester told Elmo, "point number one, ya got
my daughter pregnant, point number two, ya ain't
married to er and point number three, this shotgun
says yer gonna be!"

Proposal:

Poor ole Earl went out with Emma Jean last week
and he asked her ta marry him.
Emma Jean told him she would marry him on one
condition. She said she didn't want no damn kids.

Earl went down the very next mornin and sold off
his entire goat herd!

Well folks, I gotta git on outa here and git
something done. It was shur good talkin to ya and
maybe we can hang out agin some time!
Talk atcha later!

CPSIA information can be obtained
at www.ICGtesting.com
Printed in the USA
BVHW072305080223
658188BV00004B/45